Quotable Texas Women

Lorraine

Happy Mother's
Day 2015

Love

Jug :)

Quotable Texas Women

Susie Kelly Flatau and Lou Halsell Rodenberger

State House Press

McMurry University
Abilene, Texas

Library of Congress Cataloging-in-Publication Data

Quotable Texas women / [compiled by] Susie Kelly Flatau and
Lou Halsell Rodenberger.
p. cm.
Includes index.
ISBN 1-880510-89-8 (pbk.)
1. Women—Texas—Quotations. 2. Quotations, American—Texas.
I. Flatau, Susie Kelly. II. Rodenberger, Lou Halsell.

PN6081.5.Q59 2005
305.4'09764—dc22

2004029605

State House Press
McMurry Station, Box 637
Abilene, TX 79697-0637
(325) 793-4682
www.mcwhiney.org

Printed in the United States of America

Book designed by Rosenbohm Graphic Design

Contents

INTRODUCTION

Good quotations capture complex ideas in a few words. They inspire an "aha, that's so right" response as they convey philosophies of life, valuable advice, commentaries on friends, family and food, and witty observations about human failure and success.

In these pages, we have collected several hundred statements by Texas women, who have a long tradition of saying things that should be remembered.

Amelia Barr, who lived in Austin for a decade in the 1850s, observed, "Happiness is like religion; it is a mystery and should not be explained or reasoned about." Karen Hughes, an Austin resident of the current century, suggested, "The most important thing we do in life is to choose our loves and order them well."

Electra Waggoner Biggs recalled her mother's advice "to always be able to look at myself in the mirror with no regrets," while Artie Stockton quipped, "A good time to lie to yourself is that first look in the morning's mirror."

The first woman governor of Texas, Miriam 'Ma' Ferguson, noted, "The governor of a state needs to save money, and everybody knows a wife can always save two dollars where a husband can save only one." The next woman governor of Texas, Ann

Richards, pointed out, "There is a lot more to life than just struggling to make money."

The quotations included here cover topics as diverse as Texas itself—from Carol Rose's comment about age ("Age is just a number and mine's unlisted") to golfing legend Babe Didrikson Zaharias' formula for success in sports or anywhere else ("Practice and concentration, then more practice and more concentration") to Connie Douglas Reeves' succinct advice on independence and self-reliance ("Always saddle your own horse").

We hope these words of wit and wisdom will challenge you to think, cause you to laugh, encourage you to share them with family and friends, and help you appreciate the observation expressed by J'Nell Pate: "Money spent on a book is not wasted."

ADVENTURE

Assume the journey will be a roller coaster. Do something you love; then the hard work is just part of the exciting adventure.

Sheri McConnell

I say, follow your bliss and don't be afraid, and doors will open where you didn't know they were going to be. That's a good endorsement for taking on adventure.

Betty Sue Flowers

Adventure is something you seek for pleasure, or even for profit, like a gold rush or invading a country, . . . but experience is what really happens to you in the long run; the truth that finally overtakes you.

Katherine Anne Porter

Sometimes it takes a step backward to discover a new path.

Diane Gonzales Bertrand

All adventures, especially into new territory, are scary.

Sally Ride

Everybody ought to be climbing a mountain or doing something to get the adrenaline going. If you can't climb a mountain, you can read a book and get excited.
Clara Mounce

I was nearly fifty when I began hiking, and later, backpacking, and whenever I would get to the top of something I thought I couldn't climb, I'd swell with pride and ask myself what other hills in my life might I now take on?
Linda Ellerbee

A little stress and adventure is good for you, if nothing else, just to prove you are alive.
Lady Bird Johnson

ADVICE

Remember, nowadays you can hit the undo button and just about everything will be all right. If not, reboot; step into your boots and kick the hell out of the panic button!
Becky Chavarría-Chairez

Don't take yourself too seriously—we are likened to one grain of sand on a beach in the big picture.

Dot Woodfin

If you're going to play the game properly you'd better know every rule.

Barbara Jordan

Sing the birdsong that you were given and know that that is enough.

Susan Murray

Airplane pilots know that if you focus on the squished bugs on the windshield while you are making a take-off, you will most likely hit the big trees at the end of the runway just as you reach climb power. Same with life. You have to keep your focus on the goal in the distance, not on the obstacles between it and you.

Nancy Robinson Masters

My mother's best advice was to always be able to look at myself in the mirror with no regrets. Like a fine racehorse, never quit until you cross the finish line.

Electra Waggoner Biggs

Remember to look through the windshield and not the rear-view mirror, because you've already been there.

Leah Shaver

Be different and keep an open mind.

Becky Chavarría-Chairez

❖

Although it is accurate that our first appearance makes an impact on other people, that should not be the lasting impact.

Vivian Castleberry

❖

If you keep dipping from the sour pickle barrel, you'll never taste anything sweet.

Junette Kirkham Woller

❖

There are two choices in dealing with life. One can smile and make everyone's burden a little lighter, or one can frown and make everyone's burden even heavier. I choose to smile.

Junette Kirkham Woller

❖

I have very strong feelings about how you lead your life. You always look ahead; you never look back.

Ann Richards

❖

Idle conversation is often negative.

Guida Jackson

The first rule
of holes:
when you're
in one,
stop digging.

Molly Ivins

Don't load the wagon and forget the mule.
Era Lee Caldwell

I reflected on the flying lessons I had learned years ago that once again proved true: always have a plan, always have plenty of options, always have patience. Above all, when things go wrong, always go back to the basics. Hold heading, hold altitude, and hold on to good judgment.
Nancy Robinson Masters

AGE

As you grow old be careful with your longing to sit in the sun. The results may be that you dry up like a prune.
Larue Smith

Age is just a number and mine's unlisted.
Carol Rose

It gets harder and harder each year to look as young as I feel. The mirror is obviously working against me.
Sydney Newman Dotson

Older? It's who you've always been, only later.

Jan Epton Seale

One benefit of getting older is the boost to your social life—
all your new acquaintances (nurses, therapists, lab techni-
cians, EMTs, doctors) keep your calendar full.

Doris Lakey

They say you should act your age not your shoe size. Listen,
be the age you want to be. As for me, I like my shoe size: 7. I'd
rather have my foot in my mouth any day!

Becky Chavarría-Chairez

A major advantage of age is learning to accept people without passing judgment.

Liz Carpenter

By the time she is seventy every woman should get rid of her
washer and dryer. After all, she will benefit someone who
needs a job, keeping them in work, and set an example for
younger women everywhere. It's our responsibility as elders.

Ginnie Siena Bivona

The only difference between a rut and a grave is the depth,
and I'm not ready for either one.

Etta Moten Barnett

I like the age I am now because I have already learned so much about life. I'm calm about what happens—I don't worry. I take life as it comes.

Violette Newton

If I am fortunate enough to reach my eightieth birthday, will I be content? Only if I have had the courage to follow what I am urgently called to do, which is to express myself truthfully. The prospect of not realizing my creative potential scares me much more than my physical decline or fading beauty.

Christine Albert

The truth is, at seventy-eight, I'm a little more, "whatever happens, happens." I've had the greatest life in the world.

Barbara Bush

I want to retire to something rather than just retire.

Louise Raggio

I never talked about my age until it became something to be proud of.

Ebby Halliday

I make sure to keep current by talking to young people.

Etta Moten Barnett

Nature, eternal, cradles the echoes of our youth.

Susie Kelly Flatau

ANIMALS

I didn't want to be a stockbroker anymore. There wasn't a political campaign that interested me. I decided to train a bird dog.

Ramona Bass

I must give special tribute to my wonderful trick riding horses. They were not only fifty percent of the act, but our business partners and our best friends.

Mitzi Lucas Riley

My friends tell me when they die and go to heaven they want to come back as one of my horses.

Alice Walton

If childhood pets teach responsibility, they also teach the limits of love. To feed and to walk and to brush and to sift through the litter box, not just when you feel like it but every day, every day because this is your pet.

Marion Winik

Have you ever loved a dog? You can love a cow, too. It tears your insides out to sell them. You sit there and bawl because you had to sell a cow to make a payment.

Marjorie Hague

ART

An artist is one of the lucky ones who by fluke of family genetics, birth order, or childhood pain, hears her own inner voice and has the guts to take it seriously and follow it, not conform to the safety of doing what everyone else is doing.

Susan Murray

And what is art if it does not enchant?

Dominique De Menil

Art is the doorway to fields of grace.

Betty Sue Flowers

It helps to laugh when I recall the hurdles I've faced—and gotten over–in the art world. Being accepted as a female sculptor was one of the biggest ones. For years I wasn't accepted into art shows because I was just "one of those girls" in the eyes of most art dealers. In a man's world, sculptures of women and children are seen as weak and "namby-pamby."

Glenna Goodacre

❖

The real task of art is to bring society newly to birth, to help it transform and be reborn.

Betty Sue Flowers

❖

It has at last dawned upon the American mind that too little attention is paid to drawing and painting, and that the study of art is one of the most important of studies.

Lucy Kidd-Key

❖

One scrap of homemade fabric can tell us much about the realities and nuances of a woman's life, of a community's life, in nineteenth-century Texas.

Paula Mitchell Marks

❖

If I didn't quilt I'd go crazy. My hands have got to be busy.

Mabel Payne

ATTITUDE

If you win, be gracious. If you lose, be gracious. The important thing is that you get to strut your stuff.

Ellen Reid Smith

Attitude is everything. I accept my faith and nothing is stopping me. I know that life goes on. I know that life is precious and we need to embrace it. We must have faith.

Rita Lieu-LeNoble

I am a believer in a positive approach to problems.

Sarah T. Hughes

When feeling uncomfortable about going into a room full of people, walk in as if you own the room or you're considering purchasing it.

Molly Jo Evans

My favorite exercise: I pretend the word "no" does not exist and I do.

Becky Chavarría-Chairez

If you think you can, you're right; and if you think you can't, you're right.

Mary Kay Ash

Time has shown me that independence doesn't come from a change in geographic location. Independence is born with a change in attitudes.

Diane Gonzales Bertrand

BEAUTY

Beauty is a state of mind. Any woman of any age, weight, or fashion sense can be beautiful by believing it's so.

Etta Moten Barnett

Wallflowers are an unknown shrub in this part of the country; the men have too much gallantry to allow them to flourish, even if accidentally transplanted here from colder climes.

Teresa Griffin Vielé

A good time to lie to yourself is that first look in the morning's mirror.

Artie Stockton

BOOKS & READING

Money spent on a book is not wasted.
J'Nell Pate

❖

Some of my best friends are books.
Doris Lakey

❖

While growing up in a small town during the 50s and 60s, I was always cautioned not to wear too much makeup, dress too loudly, or wear rhinestone jewelry because people would think I was a floozy instead of a respectable and well-educated young lady. Now, as an older and hopefully wiser woman, I've given myself permission to blossom like a Texas wild flower as I celebrate life, friends and books. And I've learned that floozies can still have intelligent and in-depth discussions about the books of the month even if they put on tons of makeup, dress themselves in hot pink and leopard skin prints, tease their hair and then top it off with a glittery tiara.
Betty Kurecka

❖

Instead of just mindlessly reading for escapism or for pleasure, I want them to think.
Joy Wilson

My West Texas grandmother taught me the most important accessory for the bedroom is a reading lamp. Life is a discovery when you read a few pages of your current book, the Bible, or even a magazine story just before you fall asleep. Today I promote reading to my granddaughter by wearing a tiara as we read just before bedtime.

Wanda Horton

I have a real soft spot in my heart for librarians and people who care about books.

Ann Richards

I imagine every person who loves to read can think back on points of their life, with great nostalgia, when you remember the summer, for instance, that you read all the Russian writers.

Laura Bush

I loved to read. I remember reading any book I found about the house. Stepmother did not approve of me reading and called me a "bookworm." I knew it must be something horrid.

Mary Ann Nicholson

The physical presence of books stimulates my mind.

Betty Sue Flowers

I confess a great fondness for librarians. They are the quiet custodians of our most valuable treasure.

Evelyn Oppenheimer

A book can be wonderful and powerful and accessible and artful all at the same time.

Chitra Banerjee Divakaruni

To me a book is the ultimate vacation from life.

Kathy Patrick

CHILDREN

There's nothing more important for our country than for every child who achieves to have an avenue to success, no matter what his economic circumstance.

Ruth Simmons

There is so much goodness in the world. You can see it in the eyes of animals and of children. You can feel it when you hug a tree.

Guida Jackson

Children are apt to live up to what you believe of them.

Lady Bird Johnson

Your children themselves become teachers and pull you deeper into the essence of your being.

Betty Sue Flowers

❖

Nothing is more important than a child.

Hazel Kelley Wilson

❖

Parents teach children how TO behave on purpose and how NOT to behave quite by accident.

Ben Joyce (B.J.) Davis

❖

You have to love your children unselfishly. That's hard. But it's the only way.

Barbara Bush

❖

Sometimes God lets me hold the whole world in my arms. And he squeezes it all into a small child's hug.

Florence (Flo) Baurys

❖

Children need to understand their own history so they can understand their own world.

Ramona Bass

There are no illegitimate children, only illegitimate parents.

Edna Gladney

Kids are like horses. You give them a fence, but with enough space to run, so they don't jump out.

Helene Lee

❖

I think, like every parent, if your children are happy, then parents are happy. And if they're unhappy, then there's nothing more difficult for parents.

Laura Bush

❖

Conversation with a child is a privilege, because you can learn a thing or two.

Guida Jackson

❖

The darn trouble with cleaning the house is it gets dirty the next day anyway, so skip a week if you have to. The children are the most important things.

Barbara Bush

❖

It makes me so infuriated my hair stands up every time I hear somebody doom and doom young people. I could just tear 'em to pieces. All of them aren't bad. They're as good as they were when I came along.

Lyndal Higgs

COMMUNITY

An organization is only as strong as its component pieces. We strengthen women in an organization by making them more effective.

Sarah Weddington

We are not separate; we are one, and we have to help each other.

Patty Speier

If I have learned anything in business, in politics, in state or national government, it is that we can do nothing unless we work as a team . . . seeing the goals together, working together, able to make small compromises to gain the greatest common good.

Oveta Culp Hobby

The country telephone is something more than mere wires strung on tall poles, than receivers and mouthpieces. It is a living, vibrant thing, which welds the interests and problems of isolated communities in a way that is past understanding.

Hughie Call

Community is not a direct end, but arises as a kind of by-product when people are working for common ideals that are larger than themselves.

Betty Sue Flowers

Like many another rural community across the plains and prairies of West Texas, Pyron lives when nearly all visible traces have vanished. That it can still be seen by the discerning eye and felt by the understanding heart is due to such intangibles as community spirit, country cussedness, and the indelible stamp of place upon the human psyche.

Jane Gilmore Rushing

We might feel powerless to change the world events we are caught up in, but we are not, so long as we can sit around a table, break bread together, and have a conversation.

Patty Speier

COWGIRLS & COUNTRY LIVING

The emancipation of women may have begun not with the vote, nor in the cities where women marched and carried signs and protested, but rather when they mounted a good cowhorse and realized how different and fine the view. From the back of a horse, the world looked wider and possibilities greater.

Joyce Gibson Roach

On days when we rode on the roundups we were happy if we could stop for three drinks of water during the long day, and ecstatic if we could also have lunch along the way. Sometimes there was no time for either a drink of water or lunch. The job had to be done while there was daylight to see what we were doing.

Sandra Day O'Connor

Living on a ranch you become very self-sufficient.

Flournoy D. Mango

I wish everybody could grow up in the country! It is a good, wholesome life.

Callie Ross Bevill

Cowgirls are ordinary women who have done extraordinary things. It's a spirit they have.

Pat Riley

It didn't matter how sore or tired you were, when the band started playing and the applause started, you forgot your aches and pains and your goal was to please the crowd.

Mitzi Lucas Riley

❖

The covers as well as the contents of some western books have helped to shape public opinion that women on ranches had a lot more to offer than hot biscuits.

Joyce Gibson Roach

❖

It's an honor to be the first woman of the Supreme Court, but it will be even better when we get the second cowgirl on the Supreme Court.

Sandra Day O'Connor

❖

Those Texas women who left a legacy as feisty, capable ranch women made clear their backbones were stronger than twine string.

Lou Halsell Rodenberger

❖

We were considered people. We were not considered little girls who can't do anything. We played dolls, but were certainly good with screwdrivers, nails, and roundups, too.

Flournoy D. Mango

DEATH

We fear death, my friend Maria told me, so we laugh at it, and adorn it in gaudy colors, and give it shape in the form of macabre candies in order to hide our fear and make death palatable. It was El Día de los Muertos, the Day of the Dead.

Allana Martin

My eighty-four-year-old father was admitted to the hospital with three aneurysms that were in danger of rupture. But with other medical problems, he couldn't have surgery, so we were faced with some bad choices. We were talking to him about the fact that it might kill him, so I told him, 'I've heard good things about the other side, so it shouldn't scare you too much to think about moving there.' He laughed and said he had a lot of friends there already. It broke up a tense situation and everyone felt better.

Janna K. Brimer

Death cancels our engagements, but it does not affect the consequences of our acts in life.

Katherine Anne Porter

DREAMS

Everything you need to accomplish a dream is available to you.

Sherí McConnell

The winner of the hoop race will be the first to realize her dream, not society's dream, her own personal dream.

Barbara Bush

Most of my life's work started out in my dreams.

Cathy Bonner

My mother instilled in her children the belief that we could do anything. So, we learned to dream big and strive to realize those dreams.

Liz Carpenter

Through the use of imagination we invite the world to speak.

Betty Sue Flowers

Watch the stars burn across the galaxy, then dream a poem.

Carlyn Luke Reding

I never intended
to become a
run-of-the-mill
person.

Barbara Jordan

Dress up your lives with imagination. Don't lose that purple mantle of illusion.

Mary Louise Cecilia "Texas" Guinan

EDUCATION

Education must be balanced . . . teaching to the heart as well as the brain.

Dot Woodfin

If it hadn't been for teachers, my God, I don't know what would have happened to me.

Ruth Simmons

To a lot of parents, a school system, regardless of its plusses or minuses, is no better or worse than the teacher who is teaching your child at the moment. Parents will put up with almost anything in the bigger picture if their children have good teachers.

Joyce Gibson Roach

Do not call for black power or green power. Call for brain power.

Barbara Jordan

Education is the hallmark of democracy.

Kay Bailey Hutchison

The key to innovation is to have a command of many disciplines and hence have many perspectives.

Sherry Gillespie

We never stop learning. There is so much to be learned as we go along, and those lessons give us energy.

Sarah Weddington

The care, nurturing, and education of young children is the crux of where humanity is going.

Vivian Castleberry

43

If I could get along with adults the way I get along with children, I'd have it made. When fall comes, I'm like an old horse turned out from the fire department.

Nena Kate Ramsey Lewis

Teachers open the door; you enter it by yourself.

Loula Grace Erdman

First-graders don't cry anymore the first day of school, but mothers do.

Prudence Mackintosh

44

They were so much alike, those little one-room schools I had known, each looking as if it had been carelessly dropped in a cup of hills enclosing a Texas-sized pasture.

Stella Gipson Polk

I have seen delicate, frail little fairy-like six-year-old beings grow into clear-eyed, forward thinking magnificent women, sympathetic and helpful mothers, and honest public-spirited citizens.

Ella Hockaday

ENLIGHTENMENT

Any path around the circle of the hero's journey is open to all of us.

Betty Sue Flowers

Women have always been leaders.

Sarah Weddington

It is the nature of man to manifest his own misery.

Junette Kirkham Woller

The ability to embrace my ordinariness makes me feel extraordinary.

Jana Kennon

Anytime a person is enlightened—they become more powerful—and they become an asset to all of humanity.

Sherí McConnell

The way you overcome shyness is to become so wrapped up in something you forget to be afraid.

Lady Bird Johnson

When I was ten years old, mother had the flu. I was giving the house a once-over for Sunday and Daddy introduced me to his philosophy—"It's the corners that count." As he swept the floor he pulled out the rocking chairs, cedar chests, and tables. He even pulled out the heavy oil stove and kitchen cabinet. The room was not clean until it was swept in the corners. True with painting, polishing, gardening, shipbuilding, bookkeeping, and all other matters of life, "It's the corners that count."

Virginia Hall Irby

Laughing at yourself is the shampoo of the soul.

Artie Stockton

If I were God, I would throw a storm or two down to earth, wreak some small havoc, flail leaves about, swirl dust into already-blind eyes. That should get some attention. The flood didn't work.

Sherry Craven

Nothing like a lot of distracting saber-rattling to get you to take your eyes off the shell with the pea under it.

Molly Ivins

I can sleep anywhere. I think if you have a clean conscience and you have faith, there is no need to stay awake.

Ninfa Laurenzo

I know that the instinct that respects all life, the instinct that understands equality, survives in all of us in spite of over-whelming, unfair tradition.

Estela Portillo Trambley

My failures, and there are many, whap me on the head and give me in no uncertain terms my identity, for in my vulnera-bilities I stand most naked, most revealed, most transparent.

Sherry Craven

48

When we flew the replica Spirit of St. Louis, Verne Jobst, senior pilot for United Airlines, told me the secret to being a good tailwheel pilot was to always keep my feet and my fanny moving the same direction. I've found that philosophy works for just about everything that happens in life.

Nancy Robinson Masters

We rush, rush, rush here, rush there, and I do not see that we accomplish an extraordinary amount. Do not think for a minute that I am one who thinks the old times are best for I do not. I think we are living in the "Golden Age," but I do wonder where the time goes; it flies faster than a weaver's shuttle.

Sallie Reynolds Matthews

Fear is the static that keeps us from hearing.

Jo Virgil

FAMILY

I don't want to forget my ethnicity. Being proud of my heritage has made me a stronger human being.

Rosa R. Guerrero

Blending family with a career is like a churning kaleidoscope through which brilliant sunshine and a pallet of color are visibly sharpened, redefined, and ultimately arranged into an end product of graceful yet chaotic beauty.

Joy E. Cressler

Give the young people in your life some responsibilities and then hold them accountable.

Kathy McConnell

The family is at the heart of this world and without it, nothing is going to function very long.

Vivian Castleberry

Through the loving experience of a human family, we begin to understand the awesome privilege we have as part of the family of God.

Florence (Flo) Baurys

This is my grandmother's way—always busy plopping more mashed potatoes on your plate whether you want them or not.

Ann Whitaker

The mildew in the shower won't go anywhere if you ignore it for a day so you can pack your family up and go to a movie—or the park—or the beach—or just to the back yard to play catch.

Liz Carpenter

My father had no sons, but he made clear that girls could do anything they wanted to do—from throwing a softball straight and hard to making top grades in the classroom.

Lou Halsell Rodenberger

My father told me he thought that I would probably be a better pilot than the boys.

Florene Miller Watson

FOOD

Some say sausage making, like law making, is a process you never watch. An alternative: make sausage yourself.

Linda West Eckhardt

Almost anything can be saved with whipped cream and powdered sugar.

Rebecca Rather

My parents never turned anyone away at mealtime. Mama could stretch a meal farther than anyone I have ever known by adding more milk or water to the gravy and making the biscuits a little smaller.

Jean Flynn

Cook things so you can tell what they are. Good plain food ain't committed no crime an' don't need no disguise.

Mary Lasswell

Someone asked me once what did we take [to a family reunion], and I had to admit just seven children with hearty appetites! What could I possibly add to that spread? I wouldn't even dare.

Mary Faulk Koock

I have come to see recipes as a window through which one can learn something about people. You can learn who is generous and who is parsimonious. You can learn who has patience and who has little time. I'd swear you almost can tell who is skinny and who is fat—just by looking through a personal recipe book.

Linda West Eckhardt

We learned from our German heritage that mealtime is an important part of the day, not only for sustenance, but as a time for family and friends to keep in touch. We are ever mindful of the fact that love and care go into the preparation of food, whether the preparation takes five minutes or five hours. Then, when it is prepared, everyone, including the cook, should sit down and leisurely enjoy the meal as a celebration of life and in gratitude for the bounty on the table.

Candy Wagner and Sandra Marquez

If I am going to eat dessert, I want it to be really, really sinful.

Rebecca Rather

The dining room is one of the last outposts of civilizations.
Helen L. Corbitt

❖

When I was growing up, we ate what was on the table and then asked, "What was it?"
Jean Flynn

❖

Ranch fare is simple but intense food. The trick is to get the most flavor from the most basic of ingredients.
Dotty Griffith

FRIENDS & FRIENDLINESS

Winning has always meant much to me, but winning friends has meant the most.
Babe Didrikson Zaharis

❖

When you tie your life in knots, you can't expect your friends to always do the untying for you.
Junette Kirkham Woller

❖

My friend ain't heavy, 'cause we've been dieting for years.
Florence (Flo) Baurys

The friendliness
of Texas folks
disproves a lot of
Texas jokes.

Marianne McNeil Logan

Even after all these years of unexpected complexities, disappointments, triumphs and bad movies—when I am with my friends, why is it that I always feel so much more hopeful?

Ruth Pennebaker

Sisterhood is a sacred state of non-competition. My sisters will love me . . . warts and all.

Jennifer E. Naglieri

Up North, I was always taught the social graces. When I moved to Texas, I found out they actually practice them.

Dorene Badalamenti

GUIDANCE

You cannot take part in the fray without getting some stabs and cuts and abrasions.

Lady Bird Johnson

We have to be comfortable with who we are, regardless of who that is, because we can't be comfortable with anybody else if we're still trying to find out who we are.

Toody Byrd

When in doubt—don't

Joan R. Neubauer

You just don't luck into things as much as you'd like to think you do. You build step by step, whether it's friendships or opportunities.

Barbara Bush

❖

If you work hard enough and believe in yourself, you can accomplish any great endeavor.

Cathy Bonner

❖

ALL problems are communication problems. (It's easy to stew over technical problems and forget what the real problems are.)

Sherry Gillespie

❖

I always told my boys, "You carry your boredom with you. Don't blame it on where you are."

Sylvia Switzer

❖

Keeping the goal in mind is important, but enjoying the process along the way is crucial.

Dot Woodfin

❖

Don't let fears stop you from trying. Take risks and realize that "action" is one of the key ingredients in accomplishing goals no matter what your circumstances are.

Sheri McConnell

HAPPINESS & SIMPLICITY

Happiness is the goal of all human achievement.

Rosa R. Guerrero

The happiest people that I have known are those who look upon each day with gratitude, each trial as an opportunity, and each task as a gift.

Janell Kleberg

When the mind is present in the heart, we call it happiness.

Betty Sue Flowers

In a world where stuff means security and power, status and love, it seems impossible to have too much. And yet, when I listen to my heart, I know that real wealth lies somewhere else.

Susan Hanson

Laughter is vital as the vital signs fade.

Liz Carpenter

What can we do but laugh. It's better than crying!

Rose-Mary Rumbley

Lifetime happiness
is found in little
everyday things,
not in one big thing.

Junette Kirkham Woller

Make sure every day that you do something you like. Make a list of what's important to you. So at the end of your life, which we know passes quicker than we think, you don't have any regrets or major regrets.

Patricia Hill

In the past, life may have seemed more simple because folks had a better handle on labels–we knew what to call things.

Joyce Gibson Roach

A spirit of harmony can only survive if each of us remembers, when bitterness and self-interest seem to prevail, that we share a common destiny.

63

Barbara Jordan

I am content with the simplicity of my life.

Jana Kennon

Nothing exists you cannot do without.

Margaret Cousins

Humor requires exaggeration and an element of surprise.

Sarah Weddington

HUMOR & WIT

I don't mind if you pick up items from my coffee table to look at them . . . just please be sure to put them back on top of the same dust circle.

Jane R. Peppard

The best revenge against your detractors, as well as every corporate scoundrel, unscrupulous public official, arrogant office nurse, and pesky telephone solicitor, is to outlive them.

Guida Jackson

Never trust a person who doesn't like chocolate.

Joan R. Neubauer

We don't run errands; our errands run us.

Betty Sue Flowers

Being a dating woman is like being a bank teller . . . : NEXT!

Donna K. Martin

I dearly love the state of Texas, but I consider that a harmless perversion on my part, and discuss it only with consenting adults.

Molly Ivins

I cannot remember if we are upscaling or downsizing this year. Either way, it's going to cost us money.

Sydney Newman Dotson

I'll tell you anything you want to know. Just don't ask me my age, my weight, or the real color of my hair.

Joyce A. Dehlin

I learned early in life that humor diverts, energizes, and heals.

Liz Carpenter

I'm a member of the EA—that's exercise anonymous. If you feel like exercising, call me and I'll talk you out of it.

Mary Kay Ash

Son, when are you gonna break the factory seal on your brain? Do you think you're gonna get charged for the mileage you put on what little you got up there between your ears?

Sarah Bird

There are people who are accumulators while others are minimalists. There are those who keep and those who throw away. They usually marry each other.

Carolyn Osborn

If you can't make up
your mind,
"What the hell"
is usually the right
answer.

Ellen Reid Smith

When I was in high school I wore fringe vests and big black Stetson hats and boots and I smoked Red Dot cigars and everybody called me a weirdo. . . . When I got old and respected they called me eccentric. And hell, it's the same thing.

Annie Golightly

The president knows I'm tall—not big. We've had that conversation.

Karen Hughes

INNER STRENGTH

To revise one's thoughts or one's identity . . . didn't necessarily deliver new meaning. It was like repeating a word—troublesome, troublesome, troublesome—until the letters blurred, the sound garbled, and meaning vanished.

Jill Patterson

You can do things to me. You can bend me to the ground, but I will be just like a tree with a taproot that is extremely deep. I will stand up tomorrow and I will still be there fighting for what I believe.

Vivian Castleberry

There are a lot of people who will compromise when it's to their advantage, but I won't compromise.

Enid Mae Justin

Sometimes sacred moments emerge out of a great darkness.

Susan Wittig Albert

❖

It takes a lot of courage to enter into another's pain and be there with them.

Pat Flathouse

❖

It's not an easy road to live a genuine life.

Susan Murray

INSIGHTS

Good character is the core of everything that is worthy.

Dot Woodfin

Few in any generation want to listen; they just want to be heard.

Junette Kirkham Woller

A rotten tangerine might be a sorry judge of a collection of mixed fruit.

Jo Virgil

❖

MAYBE—Faulkner called it the best word in the language. It holds dreams, stars-in-your-eyes adventures, love and HOPE in only five letters. Maybe this will be the summer of . . . ? Maybe I will . . . ? Maybe . . .

Bettye Alexander Cook

❖

You can't rest on your laurels. People who take the bows and accept the applause and then don't do anything else, very quickly get stale and rusty.

Vivian Castleberry

❖

Foolish modesty lags behind while brazen impudence goes forth and eats the pudding.

Eleanor Brackenridge

❖

The society that we create is like a laboratory zoo worthy of continued scientific study.

Evangelina Vigil-Piñon

Strangers become just
like me–when I walked
in their shoes.

Grace Halsell

Mediocre talents always have in them an element of tragedy. Sometimes showmanship augments competence and passes for genius.

Minetta Altgelt Goyne

❖

There is a lot more to life than just struggling to make money.

Ann Richards

LEADERSHIP

Leaders, as stars, illuminate and influence in all directions.

Sarah Weddington

❖

Any committee is only as good as the most knowledgeable, determined, and vigorous person on it. There must be somebody who provides the flame.

Lady Bird Johnson

❖

I believe this is the essence of leadership—accepting responsibility for the outcome and sharing the work and the credit with others.

Kathy Whitmire

I find it mind boggling that I was hired to be a leader and empowered to make decisions—until I made a decision. I found I was not empowered at all.

Sydney Newman Dotson

Good leaders both give energy and receive it.

Sarah Weddington

I'm really glad that our young people missed the Depression and missed the great big war. But I do regret that they missed the leaders that I knew. Leaders who told us when things were tough, and that we would have to sacrifice, and these difficulties might last awhile. They didn't tell us things were hard for us because we were different, or isolated, or special interests. They brought us together and they gave us a sense of national purpose.

Ann Richards

Texans are indebted to the strong, determined women who challenged society's structure and gave us role models to follow.

Jean Flynn

The leadership instinct you are born with is the backbone. You develop the funny bone and the wishbone to go with it.

Elaine Bradley Agather

Women have always been leaders, but the women leaders of today—younger and older alike—have a unique opportunity to leave thumbprints on modern events.

Sarah Weddington

LEGACY

In the American Southwest, we have a saying for the meaning of the graffiti and mementos left throughout the centuries on cliff faces and other sites by travelers and explorers. *"Paso por aqui."* "I passed by here."

Sylvia Ann Grider

❖

We are all of us dressed in each other's silks, woven together across time and universe in a garment of existence that assures us we are not alone.

Jan Epton Seale

❖

We are still learning how to tell our cultural story through the lens of ordinary men and women and not just through the biographies of great men.

Betty Sue Flowers

Nobody had anything, but we all had plenty of nothing together in equal proportions and at the same time so that no one felt left out.

Joyce Gibson Roach

I've got a heritage that's very rich. To me it's like having a factory of diamonds.

Dora Villarreal

❖

I've loved old courthouses since I was a child in Missouri. So, when I saw these old courthouses falling down around me, I just knew something had to be done.

Shirley Caldwell

❖

Only if we know the past can we understand the present and provide for the future.

Barbara Likan

❖

This house was old fifty years ago. . . . The past lives here where nothing is thrown away.

Bonnie Bowman Korbell

❖

Live your life in such a way that you have great stories to tell.

Jo Virgil

❖

These old things have not lost their usefulness. Our memories use them. They feed our lives with love.

Bonnie Bowman Korbell

It has taken me a long time to understand that my memories largely shape the meaning of my life, and that sometimes memories are a trick you play on yourself.

Sandra Scofield

The study of the past is much more complex than once thought. As more and more evidence of the lives of individual Texas women surfaces, social historians can begin unraveling the connections between women and history.

Lois E. Myers

LIFE

Life is like the jagged line on a hospital EKG reading. When that line is flat, you're dead. So instead of trying to straighten everything out, I have learned to direct my energy toward the issues and problems that are most important.

Sarah Weddington

Socrates said that the unrecorded life is not worth living, but it may also be true that the unlived life is not worth recording.

Jan Epton Seale

I live a day at a time. Each day I look for a kernel of excitement. In the morning, I say: "What is my exciting thing for today?" Then, I do the day. Don't ask me about tomorrow.

Barbara Jordan

Remember, you are making a life, you are not making a living

Vivian Castleberry

That's all there is to life anyway–doin' what you love to do. If you can.

Jackie Worthington

I have done much talk . . .about closing circles–bringing together parts of my life that did not seem to fit at the time but as events unfolded made perfect circles and perfect closures. Many of my publishing decisions have been based upon such closures, and they have always been good.

Fran Vick

I find in life it is not so much the day but the good use we put the day.

Mrs. R. A. Winn

Life is pretty empty when the most exciting part is waiting for the junk mail.

Katherine Kirk Wilson

Life is like a bike ride . . . rough roads with bumps just make you appreciate the smooth ones. Going downhill is fun but climbing uphill makes you strong.

Jennifer E. Naglieri

I don't tend to look back. I've enjoyed just about everything I've ever done. The bad things in life you learn from, the good things you enjoy. I've never been one for looking back and reflecting–I'm too busy living.

Helen Kleberg Groves

LOVE

When you love somebody, you don't judge. You love and you forget and you forgive.

Rosa R. Guerrero

Passion stored up over time can sometimes be so powerful it just blows everyone away when delivered as a song or a speech.

Susan Murray

The most important thing we do in life is to choose our loves and order them well.

Karen Hughes

Just remember the world is not a playground but a school-room. Life is not a holiday but an education. One eternal lesson for us all: to teach us how better we should love.

Barbara Jordan

While it may be right to tell the truth, in affairs of the heart it isn't always wise.

Dulce Moore

Loving someone is more difficult than being loved. Love demands we lose some of our own heart in order to find someone else's heart.

Sherry Craven

It isn't easy to manage matters of the heart.

Carlyn Luke Reding

Every bit of love you can express is casting your bread upon the water—it will come back.

Liz Carpenter

Loving is like standing on the arid, desert floor, naked, but yet holding the belief of possibility in our hands.

Sherry Craven

Love isn't love until you give it away.

Tanya Taylor Allgood

He was living the age-old story; can't live with and can't live without.

Brenda Black White

MEN & WOMEN

The old-fashioned cowboys were the finest fellows I ever knew, loyal and true in every respect and had the greatest respect for women. They would lay down their lives if necessary for a woman.

Alma Miles

Who made the marital rule that the toilet seat has to be down? Many a marriages are ruined over this and similar idiosyncrasies. In our master bath, I make it a point to leave the seat UP (which takes less effort to do, than to complain about) and my husband and I live in beautiful harmony!

Terri E. Stingley

I believe that women have a capacity for understanding and compassion which a man structurally does not have, does not have because he cannot have it. He's just incapable of it.

Barbara Jordan

Before you're married camping is OK, after marriage my idea of camping is a black and white TV and a window unit (i.e. a cheap hotel).

Donna K. Martin

This putting of men against women or women against men leads to nothing constructive.

Minnie Fisher Cunningham

❖

Wedding anniversaries are milestones of endurance.

Junette Kirkham Woller

❖

A lot of guys didn't like being passed by a girl [race car driver]. But once they realized I was serious and was actually willing to do what it took to compete, most of them softened their attitudes considerably.

Mary Houge

My husband says
he can read me like
an open book.
The only problem is
he doesn't know
what page I'm on.

Sydney Newman Dotson

If men can run the world, why can't they stop wearing neckties? How intelligent is it to start the day by tying a little noose around your neck?

Linda Ellerbee

I keep thinking that these sons will outgrow the need to be punching or kicking each other, but grown men have admitted to me that they still greet their brothers by frogging them in the arm or knuckling each other on the head. That's the hard part for a female to grasp.

Prudence Mackintosh

My husband worries about immortality. I worry about next week.

Ruth Pennebaker

Let a woman make one little mistake and it becomes a joke for years.

Hallie Crawford Stillwell

I couldn't understand why some of them thought a man should be the only one that should vote. They would say, 'Well, my man does the deciding for me.' Well, my man didn't do the deciding for me. We agreed on that.

Emma Keen

MOTHERS & GRANDMOTHERS

We finish what our mothers before us start, and what we do not finish, our daughters surely will. So don't mess with Texas women—or our daughters to come.

Jan Jarboe Russell

Why, of course, my mother inspired me! Of course. She did a lot of handwork. I never did see her sit down unless she had something to do with her hands. Either crocheting, or mendin', or doing something. She was always doing something with her hands.

Frieda Williamson

Motherhood is kin to sainthood . . . both take years to accomplish and you gotta be able to work a few miracles.

Jennifer E. Naglieri

Usually daughters do not join organizations that mothers found. Every generation of women has to do it for themselves.

Vivian Castleberry

My mom raised six girls. I cannot tell you how many times I heard her say, 'You can choose to do whatever you want in life, as long as it is not immoral, illegal or blasphemy! But you're not leaving my house dressed like THAT!'

Rena Arnold

Go visit your grandmother, drink tea, listen. Return to the roots of all you know, and see faces reflecting your chin, your eyes, your hair. Follow the wandering tribes through fertile forests of green centuries to break the limit of time's prison, and fling yourself to today—claim what you are and inherit the collective wisdom.

Sherry Craven

There's a secret side to everyone's life and it wasn't until years later that I realized that all my striving, my trying to be the "Renaissance woman" was my trying to achieve the kind of love I could never get from my mother.

Carol Lane

It is a mother's job to praise and encourage and let the rest of the world take care of the criticism.

Guida Jackson

Without words, without anything but his own intelligence, beauty, and openness to the world, my fearless baby changed every day. He needed me in a direct, unmeditated, and passionate way. What he needed, I could give and I did, and so I changed too, into a grown person in the world who had responsibilities and carried them out, who made decisions for her child and saw them through, who could care for someone else completely.

Laura Furman

My grandmother, as wise a person as I've ever known, had a global view of the human condition. "The only way the world will change for the better is that everybody in the world gets tired of things being messed up," she said. "And there's not much chance of that happening."

Sunny Nash

My mother used to say, "I'm so dry I'm spittin' cotton."

Judyth Rigler

If we don't write the stories of our childhood for our grandchildren, they will not know what it was like for us.

Pat Flathouse

Most women share one common dilemma: the guilt of not being a 'perfect mother.'

Juliet Villarreal Garcia

Mothers teaching their daughters how to quilt transmitted family stories for those daughters to remember and cherish enough to pass on to their daughters a generation hence, and so down even into our day of polyester and store-bought quilt kits. For many today, the stories mean more than the souvenir antique quilts do.

Sylvia Ann Grider

MUSIC & DANCE

Music makes me feel alive, young, wild and unleashes the real me—the real me at every age. Music takes me to the thens and nows and the could-a-beens. Music is the ultimate muse.

Becky Chavarría-Chairez

Whenever I take my guitar and start to sing, I feel happy.

Lydia Mendoza

It's fashionable now to like what everyone calls "country music," but if you had to sit out in the VFW and listen to it, you'd get pretty tired of the music and the country.

Carolyn Osborn

Friends don't let friends play to empty rooms.

Connie L. Williams

I can sing songs from memory for hours. I don't have to be looking at them. I have them here in my head.

Lydia Mendoza

No one seems to think about the fact that I'm a woman [symphony orchestra conductor]. Gender doesn't affect you at all.

Marianna Gabbi

When all else fails, wear black. Learn the Argentine Tango. It does not disappoint.

Marilyn Gilbert Komechak

Dance, preferably the waltz. Wear a full skirt and whirl a lot.

Sherry Craven

The spirit soars freely when you dance with a child. In that suspended moment, self-consciousness flies away on the wings of youth.

Susie Kelly Flatau

MYTH & LORE

The future is created by the stories we tell about who we are and where we are going.

Betty Sue Flowers

As you move through life, you experience a unique journey filled with many paths—paths of success and failure, of glory and despair, of luck and misfortune. You encounter friends and family, guides and nemeses. And all contribute to your unique myth. It is that myth which must be recorded—one word at a time, one sentence at a time, one paragraph at a time.

Susie Kelly Flatau

Our stories are important. By telling them, by telling our real, true woman's story, we will challenge and correct all the myths and made-up stories about women's lives.

Susan Wittig Albert

When we incorporate ideas and issues about gender and move the study of women from periphery to center, we rearrange old stories and redefine familiar terms.

Nancy Baker Jones

Myths do not just emerge full-blown, like Athena from the head of Zeus. They're made up of bits and pieces of other myths—and the Texas myth is made up of bits and pieces of the hero myth.

Betty Sue Flowers

I began to understand that all Texas is an eternal synthesis of past and present, superimposed one upon the other. It produces a feeling of being in two places at once.

Mary Lasswell

Myth has always been male. Forever, men have sat around and talked, and, yes, even gossiped. That's where mythology comes from.

Beverly Stoeltje

It came home to me that each of us carries within him an imperishable core of regional memory.

Mary Lasswell

Told long enough, or granted enough significance, stories became myth, and myth becomes the psyche of culture, the commonly held knowledge by which a culture defines and describes itself and its members.

Nancy Baker Jones

Heroism exists only within a storytelling community. Without storytelling, heroism becomes a cultural impossibility.

Betty Sue Flowers

The myth of Texas is undeniably masculine. Say "Texas" and what comes to most people's minds is cowboys and Indians—lusty trail drivers of the sort depicted by Larry McMurtry in his Pulitzer Prize-winning novel *Lonesome Dove*—brawny oil field workers yearning to "bring in a big'un"—football players giving their all for the glory of the team.

Suzanne Comer

Few former farm people wax nostalgic about the old days. No one misses the near-starvation, the shacks, the rags that sometimes passes for clothing.

Rebecca Sharpless

NATURE

Americans are loving their national parks to death.

Melody Webb

To have grown up surrounded by nature, I know how healing it can be – chatter of birds, rattle of crickets, whoosh of wind, gurgle of water, green everywhere.

Susan Murray

Experiencing the solitude that nature provides is a form of meditation that calms the soul and purges the stress from your life.

Sherí McConnell

A wedge of geese flying from horizon to horizon, their migrant cry, a certain shade of green seen rarely in the evening sky–these are a few of the sights and sounds that give me the wondrous feeling.

Bertha McKee Dobie

Gardening is a gentle passion that quenches me physically, spiritually, and emotionally. On my knees I drink up the smell of the fertile ground as I dig holes and plant seeds alive with potential. I am a partner with God/Goddess as I nurture my adopted plants and I feel quietly satisfied at the end of my day's work.

Christine Albert

The world around you becomes your repose and your sort of spiritual something from which you draw strength and pleasure and relaxation and delight.

Lady Bird Johnson

❖

After the storm there is a soft breeze, and with shadow there is light. A caterpillar breaks its bonds with the earth but carries another life along, toward its end.

Betsy Berry

❖

The Mountain Pink is one of the most dependable fever medicines known to early settlers. . . . The plants are collected while still in blossom, dried in the air, then soaked in good brandy, and a tablespoon is given the patient three times daily.

Ellen D. Schultz

❖

The ride, through the fresh dewy morning hours! Oh, that was worth something! Everything looked as if it were "made." The sky had that wonderful blueness I have never seen anywhere but in San Antonio; the hillsides were green with the tender green of spring and there was a perfect blaze of flowers everywhere.

Mollie E. Moore Davis

Of all things in nature, sunrises appeal to me most. I feel like with a new day there is great opportunity.

Connie Douglas Reeves

The sky is so much larger here and the stars like diamonds
God spilled from a cup. They fill the heavens.

Janice Woods Windle

The power of water. It softly flows wherever it wants – into
tiny crevices, across continents. Soothing, yet it can break
down rock, erode away land. Patient, gentle, timeless.

Susan Murray

Some days are just right for going slow in the fragrance of
flowers. Other days are right for racing but who can smell the
flowers when you are sucking air?

Jennifer E. Naglieri

PASSAGES

I'll admit that I do pick up an occasional women's magazine
to read about the latest demystifying expose on
menopause—I call it wedopause. Why? Because menopause
is never all about you—it's about everybody in your world—
you, him, the kids—the we!

Becky Chavarría-Chairez

I never met a birthday I didn't like.

Bettye Alexander Cook

Some folks think of 'in between' as something to be endured on the way to somewhere else. Yet, there are wonderful lessons to be learned in that uncomfortable spot. A rainbow is only visible when you are standing in between the sunshine and the rain.

Susan Fisher Anderson

PATIENCE, PERSEVERANCE & PRUDENCE

Patience is about waiting and watching, giving our sometimes hyperactive egos the time to slip back into alignment with out hearts.

Patty Speier

❖

If I had any more patience, I would be a doctor!

Tanya Taylor Allgood

❖

To advance and lead, we must dare to go a little faster than we can control. We must also learn to get back up when we fall.

Sarah Weddington

My capacity for growth is equal only to my capacity to make mistakes.

Guida Jackson

Perseverance is the crucial ingredient to success.

Sheri McConnell

❖

The lulls along the road are chances to gather provisions for the steep climb ahead.

Guida Jackson

❖

CAN'T, never did anything; if you want to succeed, you have to CAN.

Roberta Britt

❖

Aerodynamically the bumblebee shouldn't be able to fly, but the bumblebee doesn't know that so it goes on flying anyway.

Mary Kay Ash

❖

I developed a trait that has stood me in good stead all my life; just plain, mule-headed persistence.

Enid Mae Justin

❖

I believe in practicing prudence at least once every two or three years.

Molly Ivins

PEACE & WAR

Our veterans deserve the support of a grateful nation.

Mary Ellen Ancelin Guay

❖

I would have gone into combat if I'd been ordered to.

Dorothy A. Lucas

❖

Let the generations know that women in uniform also guaranteed their freedom. That our resolve was just as great as the men who stood among us.

Anonymous, Army nurse in World War II

❖

There is no peace without surrender.

Guida Jackson

❖

I'm working for a day when war is obsolete.

Frances (Sissy) Farenthold

❖

For me, there is only one question: Are you a peacemaker or a peacekeeper?

Becky Chavarría-Chairez

❖

War is not nice.

Barbara Bush

PIONEER WOMEN

One thing that can be said of the women of the Old South.
They faced defeat and changed conditions with a high
courage. What they did not know they felt they could learn,
which fact has been proved long ago.

Florence Lanham

Work never killed anybody. From the time I married on, my
life was busy. I didn't realize what all I had done, but my life
is well spent.

Odyne Jones

She used to tell how when they came finally to the home-
stead and the wagon stopped, she felt so lonely. There was an
emptiness as far as the eye could see. How could a human
endure?

Odessa Wilmon

We learned almost all that we ever did know about practical
living from our friends on the high prairies of Texas.

Seigniora Russell Laune

The wind was the cause of it all. The sand, too, had a share in it, and human beings were involved, but the wind was the primal force, and but for it the whole series of events would not have happened.

Dorothy Scarborough

The vermin, the famine, hot winds and dry soil, which caused clouds of dust to fill the sultry air in July and August and lodge on everything, made me begin to think . . . that it would have been better to remain in New Orleans and keep thread and needle store than go to Texas.

Teresa Griffin Vielé

The pioneers must push; they need to be men of action. The cowards who run away seldom run to dangers; hence it is safe to say that not many cowards came to Texas in the early days.

Sister M. Agatha Sheehan

God grant that my experience may never be yours.

Olive Oatman Fairchild

The Texas frontier dared its women to adhere to society's rules and then threw in their way every conceivable obstacle: Indians, heat, blue northers, bugs, wind, isolation, and violence.

Sherrie S. McLeroy

Living in a wild country under circumstances requiring constant exertion, forms the character to great and daring enterprise. Women thus situated are known to perform exploits, which the effeminate men of populace cities might tremble at.

Mary Austin Holley

Taking all things together, the life lived by the women of Austin at that date [1856] was a joyous, genial existence. . . . Their chief employment appeared to be an endless tucking of fine muslin and inserting lace in same. . . . Some of the women chewed snuff without cessation and such women neither "tucked" nor "inserted."

Amelia Barr

The Texas woman was, when I knew her, more than half a century ago, brave and resourceful, especially when her environment was anxious and dangerous. They were then nearly without exception fine riders and crack shots, and quite able, when the men of the household were away, to manage their ranches or plantations, and keep such faithful guard over the families and household, that I never once in ten years, heard of any Indian, or other tragedy occurring.

Amelia Barr

They say it was Harvey Girls that settled the West. I guess in some way that's true.

Rose Farshon

POLITICS

The power I exert on the court depends on the power of my arguments, not on my gender.

Sandra Day O'Connor

Politics is not a picture on a wall or a television sitcom that you can decide you don't much care for.

Molly Ivins

I'm not a feminist in any sense of the word. I'm a citizen with, I hope, a sense of responsibility.

Oveta Culp Hobby

I hate politics. I am not a politician. I like to tell it like it is. I like to be up front with people. Half the people are mad at you all the time. You don't get paid. It's a very hard job. But I care very much about our country. I want to keep the specialness of this area.

Diane Lacy

The stakes are much too high for government to be a spectator sport.

Barbara Jordan

Ideals of responsibility, community, and the common good are absolutely necessary for the health of the civic spirit.

Betty Sue Flowers

The rule was that girls never ran for [student council] president at Austin High—only vice-president. Well, I reversed that order, and I asked a cheerleader friend of mine—a male—to be my running mate.

Carole McClellan

I don't know what it is about cows and sexism, but the two go together. I used to breathe a sigh of relief when I got out of cow country.

Frances (Sissy) Farenthold

Human rights is not a temporary or transitory political issue. We have got to respect the humanity of each other and know that no one has the right to rule others.

Barbara Jordan

At a dinner party, something serious would come up and the glaze would come over the men's eyes when you spoke up, like they were thinking, "Oh my God, the bimbo's at it again."

Chris Miller

The governor of a state needs to save money, and everybody knows a wife can always save two dollars where a husband can save only one.

Miriam 'Ma' Ferguson

I decided I could certainly run and lose and live with it. But if I didn't run because it would be uphill all the way—and if I threw in the towel because it was going to be tough—I could not live with that.

Carole Keeton Strayhorn

When you look at the important huddles, the important power positions, the people the big legislation is taken to and who gets all the big [campaign] checks, they're all men.

Eddie Bernice Johnson

I do not think that the founding fathers intended faithful execution of the laws to encompass death of legislation by execution.

Barbara Jordan

POTENTIAL

I get from the soil and spirit of Texas the feeling that I, as an individual, can accomplish whatever I want to, and that there are no limits, that you can just keep going, just keep soaring. I like that spirit.

Barbara Jordan

If you are politically inclined, you may be President of the United States.

Barbara Jordan

❖

Every expert in this world started out as a beginner.

Suzann Thompson

❖

It helps to know that as you let go of the strings that tie you to your past and relieve yourself of the burdens of your memories, you will be more free to meet your future.

Judy Miller

❖

I feel if you get in there and work hard and do your job, there's nothing that can hold you back.

Mary Marsh

❖

I don't want to forget that there is a potential renaissance in all of us, whoever we are.

Rosa R. Guerrero

❖

My generation has the idea that everything is possible, which is different from our parents' notion that anything is possible.

Regina Segovia

Instead of looking at life as a narrowing funnel, we can see it ever widening to choose the things we want to do, to take the wisdom we've learned and create something.

Liz Carpenter

If human beings are perceived as potentials rather than problems, as possessing strengths instead of weaknesses, as unlimited rather than dull and unresponsive, then they thrive and grow to their capabilities.

Barbara Bush

I know the value of getting good minds together to think. I have found you can move mountains when you have an army marching along with you.

Juliet Villarreal Garcia

It is amazing how even the most humble person views himself when you help him look into his past and identify some of the contributions he has made to the world around him and the people he has touched in his walk through life.

Ada Simond

RELATIONSHIPS

Everyone has an invisible sign hanging from their neck saying, "Make me feel important." Never forget this message when working with people.

Mary Kay Ash

Each person's life is unique, and every relationship is unique. A deep friendship (which a successful marriage is) is like one of the Hill Country oak trees—majestic, hardy, but a bit gnarled from adapting to conditions.

Jo Virgil

Photographs help us stay connected with those we love and allow us to revisit the important and special times in our lives.

Era Lee Caldwell

❖

Relationships built on pretense are not worth the time they take out of your life.

Junette Kirkham Woller

❖

soulmates come and go / talking of time and its long parade

Carlyn Luke Reding

At the end of your life, you will never regret not having passed one more test, winning one more verdict, or not closing one more deal. You will regret time not spent with a husband, a child, a friend, or a parent.

Barbara Bush

It is only with you that I become a responsible person in the world. Only you can see the back of my neck and, therefore, reveal to me parts of my self I could not know otherwise.

Kathryn Minyard Frost

Remember that forgiving someone doesn't mean NOT feeling hurt or angry or betrayed—it simply means that you are willing to not hold on to those things. Forgiveness helps provide a cleansing.

Jo Virgil

Carrying around an emotional burden for months or years is debilitating both emotionally and physically. To be able to reconcile and forgive relieves that burden.

Beverly Williams-Hawkins

I don't look at forgiveness as conceding, but rather as letting go and freeing your soul and body from the stress that comes with resentment.

Beverly Williams-Hawkins

SELF RELIANCE

There's more than one way to go up a mountain.

Louise Raggio

❖

In polite words I told them to get lost. This company is my life and I aim to keep on running it.

Enid Mae Justin

❖

I knew I would be responsible for my own success and my own failure.

Sandra Haynie

❖

The script I am living is finally my own.

Linda Pace

❖

Poverty is not pretty. But learning how to survive can make you a stronger person.

Ruth Simmons

❖

Using your intuition allows you the ability to look internally, find the answers and the strength to be bold and act on your inner guidance.

Sherí McConnell

Always saddle your own horse.

Connie Douglas Reeves

SERVICE

Undervaluing service—whether reflected in our lack of support for full-time single mothers or the steady decline of teachers' salaries in relation to those of other professionals—will continue to have a debilitating effect on communities.

Betty Sue Flowers

Giving expands you. Life is more rewarding, more treasured, more valued, because you have chosen to give some of your blessings back.

Luci Baines Johnson

Whether it's small gestures that cost us nothing or large commitments of time and money, the opportunities to make a good difference are all around us.

Marsha Sharp

Always try to make personal connections with the people you meet. Be willing to listen and to help others. When we create a passion through serving others we are exponentially rewarded.

Sherí McConnell

How much we care is shown by how much we share.
Katherine Kirk Wilson

❖

I know charitable institutions are a godsend to those in need, but I honestly believe it is the volunteers that benefit the most.
Kelly Pace Bradley

❖

Practice giving more than you take, listening more than you talk, comforting more than you cry. By giving bits of yourself, you grow larger.

Jo Virgil

❖

The people we like best are oxygen givers. They're the leaders: the ones who give to family and friends, colleagues and clients.

Sarah Weddington

❖

Some people give time, some money, some their skills and connections, some literally give their life's blood. But everyone has something to give.

Barbara Bush

Every person has the ability to do something the world needs.

Louise Raggio

Actually growing things brings a peculiar satisfaction difficult to replicate in any other activity. Growing a patch of petunias, ditch of daisies, or a reverie of roses—turning bare dirt into beauty—fulfills a need most of us have. Having a brown thumb precludes my being of use in the garden, but I find joy in helping human beings grow

Bettye Alexander Cook

To belong to a hunk of land, a bit of soil, as if an arm or leg attached to a body, that is a gift. I have discovered that it is only in connection that we learn to be whole, and it is only in others that we discover ourselves. The gifts are in the middle of the giving.

Sherry Craven

Giving frees us from the familiar territory of our own needs by opening our mind to the unexplained worlds occupied by the needs of others.

Barbara Bush

You give your wealth, your work, your wisdom—you give those things at different times of your life. There's always a way to be useful.

Luci Baines Johnson

SPIRITUALITY & FAITH

The spiritual life is essentially a life of awakening to the possibility of choice.

Patty Speier

God exists in some form, maybe wearing a navy blue blazer and khakis, or maybe he is a she, or an "it," a force like thousands of tiny lights. Maybe he-she-it rides the wind and whispers to us all day. All I know is that there is more to life than what I can see. I plan to be open to it.

Sherry Craven

The source of resonating peace and contentment that undergirds everything else is my Christian faith.

Marsha Sharp

Grace abounds in the presence of meaningfulness.

Betty Sue Flowers

My church is in nature. I can go sit on the banks of the river and watch the water and feel the wind, and I am closer to God—or whoever runs the universe.

Connie Douglas Reeves

At the trial, I put my hand on the Bible and swore to tell the truth "so help me God." When I bowed my head to pray, the judge said, "Don't do that, it's unlawful."

Pat Capps Mehaffey

❖

Heaven is a place where poets get to sigh all they want to.

Jan Epton Seale

❖

Spirituality is about experiencing all things natural—our earth, our body, our soul, and all living creatures on this planet and beyond—in a positive way.

Sherí McConnell

❖

It is the turmoil of life that offers us the venue for spiritual growth.

Jo Virgil

❖

After 9/11, many non-profit groups adopted the "Mother Teresa budget—three pennies and God." I encourage you today to take your three pennies and do all that God has for you to do; with that in your heart, you have everything you need.

Melody Kohout

If God thinks you're wrong, it matters not who thinks you're right.

Ben Joyce (B.J.) Davis

You can appreciate one's religion and one's dedication to that religion, although you may not believe yourself what that individual is practicing.

Lillian Dunlap

God is where love is
A touch a smile a kind word
In loving the unlovely for loves sake

Jennifer E. Naglieri

I want to seek the grail in the middle of a lonely lake, to walk on water and fish for love, drop my line into some tenderness, be cooled, cleansed, created anew. I want Holy.

Sherry Craven

Mama loved Baptist revivals, not for the religion–she had quite enough of that in her own church–but for the drama.

Mary King Rodge

Life would be pedestrian and prosaic if God did not continue all of our lives to surprise our hearts with glimpses of the hereafter reflected in nature's miracles and in human love and grace.

Lou Halsell Rodenberger

❖

Did you see the preacher smiling? He wants us to think of the place we're going to where people's laws is the same as God's laws.

Jane Gilmore Rushing

❖

Pride and style have taken the place of religion.

Mrs. Talitha Wilson English

❖

Go to a brush arbor revival some Sunday and listen to the reverence with which [West Texans] sing, "Shall We Gather at the River" or "Roll Jordan, Roll." It's not heaven for which they long; it's pure fresh sweet water.

Jane Roberts Wood

❖

Whatever community of faith we may belong to, our sense of connectedness, and therefore of meaningfulness, increases when we are embedded in a larger story.

Betty Sue Flowers

SPORTS

The formula for success is simple: practice and concentration, then more practice and more concentration.

Babe Didrikson Zaharias

You can't win them all—but you can try.

Babe Didrikson Zaharias

Even before there were teams for women to play on, I believe Texas women possessed those qualities that would make them winners, regardless of scoreboard measures.

Jody Conradt

Great champions have an enormous sense of pride. The people who excel are those who are driven to show the world and prove to themselves just how good they are.

Nancy Lopez

The task of taking one's body, mind and spirit through the mighty marathon parallels the crucible of life.

Lisa Lynam

It's not just enough to swing at the ball. You've got to loosen your girdle and let 'er fly.

Babe Didrikson Zaharias

The coaching profession is a unique arena to impact lives.
Marsha Sharp

The true winners can be found in those who test themselves and move through the arduous journey with resolve, purpose and vitality despite fears, inevitable challenges and failures, and know it's not about how swift, how powerful, how attractive, but about how one endures with grace and love.
Lisa Lynam

Before I was ever in my teens, I knew exactly what I wanted to be when I grew up. My goal was to be the greatest athlete that ever lived.
Babe Didrikson Zaharias

If you win through bad sportsmanship, that's no real victory.
Babe Didrikson Zaharias

STILLNESS

While we're sleeping, the body repairs itself and grows. In fact, all growth takes place in silence.
Guida Jackson

Spare time is the connective tissue between the bones of our appointments; moments that flex and compress so our over-scheduled skeleton can curl into a ball or leap arch-backed toward the sun.

Mónica Gomez

I have been feeling little joy and enthusiasm for my daily life lately. In a period of meditation I realized that perhaps by consciously deciding each day to choose joy and enthusiasm and to notice scenes, actions of others and incidents which reinforced the two that my attitude and feelings could change. Doing this has helped.

Nancy Snyder

The simple, quiet times in my life give me the strength to deal with the more difficult times.

Jana Kennon

If you yearn for more faith, if you want answers, you must begin by listening. You must be still and listen.

Rena Pederson

Stillness sweeps into the soul when sunlight ices the tops of trees.

Susie Kelly Flatau

If you go there alone, late on a day in the springtime, you find a haven of stillness and joy. The stillness is almost like silence, but is in truth made up of countless sounds coming out of the cemetery plant life and the surrounding ranch pasture like part of the soft blessing air: a diapason of mingled high notes from insects and small birds—wrens, sparrows, finches, all the little brown birds that hide anonymously away in bushes and tall grass.

Jane Gilmore Rushing

We can't learn when we are making safe choices or choices others direct us to make. And we must get quiet and listen to discover that courage comes from the heart.

Sherí McConnell

People who cannot live with quiet have not yet learned to live with themselves.

Junette Kirkham Woller

SUCCESS

How is success measured? By the amount of passion one experiences in life.

Sherí McConnell

Female children need to be instructed about self-fulfillment and encouraged to succeed at whatever they attempt—as we individually succeed, we need to bring other women along with us.

Dr. Catalina E. "Hope" Garcia

Greatness is everywhere. It surrounds us every day, in everything we see. It hides in the accomplishments of ordinary people, passing unnoticed, in little things like barbecue.

Lisa Wingate

There are very rarely any shortcuts to lasting success.

Marsha Sharp

Success means you have found your niche and used your best efforts to try to solve the problems.

Louise Raggio

The road of success
is always under
construction!

Leah Shaver

Don't let someone who never made a takeoff keep you grounded. Be aware that as long as you don't succeed, there are those around who will feel successful.

Nancy Robinson Masters

The ladder of success is measured by the steps which go both ways—upward and downward. Always remember where you started and how you got there.

Leah Shaver

TEXAS WOMEN

Texas women are like snowflakes. Individually, they might be pretty, but together, they can stop traffic.

Cathy Bonner

Generations of Texas women have shaped history leading with distinction and determination.

Anita Perry

There's just something about women. We can do anything.

Patsy Bruner Palmquist

Somewhere, deep down,
I really feel that every
Texas woman ought
to own a pair of
red boots—even if she
never wears them.

Betty Sue Flowers

Texas women are true enigmas. They can be well educated and still speak Texan, or they can wear an evening gown or Levi's to a gala and still be respected.

Bonnie Cerace

We are metamorphosed Texans, out of our larval cocoons with wings pumped dry. Neither time nor space can hinder our adventures. We are ready to fly!

Evelyn Cook

As a woman, I have the right, no less than a man, to say and to prove that I value the reasons for living above mere life.

Grace Halsell

Women make a difference in the public arena. Women look out for the needs of women and children, the elderly and the poor.

Kathy Whitmire

I'd like to live long enough to see people not be surprised by the fact that a woman succeeded in something.

Oveta Culp Hobby

I am Woman—
hear me roar...
Or is that my
vacuum cleaner?

Liz Carpenter

Texas ladies have too much history. We carry our whole lives around on the tip of our tongues. Dancing backwards is not easy.

Connie L. Williams

They have been called "gentle tamers," though some of the more outrageous women of Texas would probably have disdained being called "gentle" anything.

Sherrie S. McLeroy

Mostly, Texas women are tough in some very fundamental ways. Not unfeminine, nor necessarily unladylike, just tough.

Molly Ivins

There is an attitude in Texas that makes you feel that you can do anything you want to do. I admire so many women who have come out of Texas and done well. I like the image Texas brings to mind–that of bigness, of strength, of goodness.

Ninfa Laurenzo

The women of Texas, like the women of every geographical division of the globe, and in every age of the world, have played their part in the drama of human progress.

Elizabeth Brooks

TOLERANCE

One thing is clear to me: We, as human beings, must be willing to accept people who are different from ourselves.

Barbara Jordan

Tolerance begets tolerance; allow others their freedom to explore life and they will be more likely to accept your wanderings, too.

Jo Virgil

We are interested in one race, the human race.

Edna Gladney

How do we create a harmonious society out of so many kinds of people? The key is tolerance—the one value that is indispensable in creating community.

Barbara Jordan

The United States was not born in harmony, much less unanimity, but with the full, exciting play of free thought and free speech. In the greatness of our heritage, we must be able to disagree without malice or hatred or ugly distortions.

Oveta Culp Hobby

TRULY TEXAS

I know I belong to a Texas country church, because the only time I lock my car or pick-up in the parking lot is during the summer so my neighbors can't leave me a bag of squash!

Anne Terry

Maybe the heat . . . maybe the jalapenos . . . maybe the cow-boys . . . something ignited my passion to move to Texas.

Rose Potter

It has been my consistent experience that the people of Texas are the warmest, friendliest, and best people anywhere.

Dee B. Whittlesey

When I married a Texas Bubba, I learned some major life les-sons—a pickup is a truck; a long neck is a beer; chili does not have beans; don't go dancing in sandals; na-a-sty has three syllables and so does Te-ex-as.

Sue Lorenz

When we moved to Texas from Kansas on July 15, 1994, the temperature was 110+. As I stood in my drive way watching the heat rise, I thought to myself, "Life as I know it is surely over." I didn't know the half of it. This is a great place to live—heat and all.

Melody Kohout

One poignant example of growing up in Texas was the time I was eleven and I got my first kiss from a boy. The pre-kiss arrangements were endless. There was much discussion of time and place. It was almost like a committee meeting.

Terrell Maverick Webb

I was always proud about being from Texas and, you know, maybe that was part of fearlessness. I love the fact that Texas is so big, but you don't feel small because of that.

Sissy Spacek

I have fished for crawdads with a string and fatback in a mud tank on the way to North Zulch; I have barrel-raced at Snook, and I have drunk sour mash whiskey from a water glass in a dance hall in Rocksprings. But the most Texas thing I ever did was swim the Navasot on horseback during a flood.

Ann Melvin

If Texas were a sane place, it wouldn't be nearly as much fun.

Molly Ivins

The image says we are tough; reality shows us we can be vulnerable. The legends tell of our openness; fact demonstrates we can be closed-minded. The motto touts us as friendly; we are, though not necessarily intimate. What we are is different—from the myths we chase, from the other women we honor, and from one another. The Texas Experience allows us that individuality.

Linda Moore-Lanning

Your Texas is no different than my Texas.

Pat Mora

VALUES

Gratitude goes deeper and lasts longer than merely being thankful.

Cindy Weigand

The majority of the American people still believe that every single individual in this country is entitled to just as much respect, just as much dignity, as every other individual.

Barbara Jordan

A lot of these people with old frontera traditions still act like money and dignity can never go together.

Naomi Shihab Nye

For me the question was: Do I advance myself as a person for the sake of personal gain or do I advance so I can make a difference?

Lydia Camarillo

Before being black, brown, or white you are a human being. Pride begins in your self.

Rosa R. Guerrero

There is no quick way to gain back broken trust, if at all.

Dot Woodfin

WISDOM

You can't build a reputation on what you intend to do.

Liz Smith

You can't make a man see if he is convinced he is blind.

Susan Fisher Anderson

Often behind a verbal barb is a knife poised to be plunged and twisted.

Junette Kirkham Woller

Some of what seem to be the worst tragedies can turn out to be the most significant things in your life.

Louise Raggio

Be careful who or what you trust. Don't pick up rats by the tail to save them from the cat . . . they'll bite you every time.

Helen Kleberg Groves

Life is short; kitchen duty is long.

Jan Epton Seale

It's odd that you can get so anesthetized by your own pain or your own problem that you don't quite fully share the hell of someone close to you.

Lady Bird Johnson

Everybody to their own taste, said the old woman as she kissed the cow. (an East Texas saying passed down from my grandmother to my mother and then to me and my sister.)

Martha Ragsdale

We have a tendency to focus on the nouns of life, when the verbs are what's real.

Guida Jackson

A buen hambre no hay mal pan.
To a good appetite no bread is bad. Hunger is the sauce.
Soledad Pérez

I have finally learned in my almost sixty years the following three things: no one else is as proud of your new car as you are; no one else thinks your children or grandchildren are as cute and smart as you do; and your problems are not nearly as important to anyone else as they are to you.
Mary Ann Ward

It's one thing I have to learn over and over and over as I do different things, that you never start where you want to be.
Vivian Castleberry

The corporate world does not always feed your eager souls. You have to feed your own souls outside of your professions.
Liz Carpenter

It has taken me years to learn that I cannot take good care of others unless I first take good care of myself!
Pat Flathouse

In the world, it's certainly an uncertain thing to know what's right.

Lady Bird Johnson

The best bread is made from cookie dough.

Ben Joyce (B.J.) Davis

Never have shrill negative attacks or name-calling educated a child, created a job, cut property taxes or solved a problem.

Carole Keeton Strayhorn

How could we be socially elevated? I cherish the good old American belief that if you are born gentlefolk, no amount of worldly honors can make you anything more, and only your own conduct makes you anything less.

Ellen Maury Slayden

I shall never forget the horror of dark mountains that foolish talk from little mole hills make.

Lexie Dean Robertson

WOMEN'S RIGHTS

Life would have been tranquil if I'd just kept my mouth shut.
Catherine Jean Crier

I have long advocated women's greater participation in politics and having them stand for office and trying to get them appointed to office. There's not nearly enough participation by women in government or in business for that matter.
Sarah T. Hughes

I thought women had come a long way until I reached the boardroom and discovered I was the only female in the room. I learned quickly that we have only just begun.
Sydney Newman Dotson

With the beginning of the third millennium, people are recognizing that it is time that we say that women's contributions are valuable.

Cathy Bonner

To deny we need and want power is to deny that we hope to be effective.

Liz Smith

We have more power over our story than we think.

Betty Sue Flowers

Freedom doesn't mean we can go willy-nilly through life only pursuing what pleases us. With freedom comes responsibility; responsibility for how we conduct ourselves, responsibility for consideration for others.

Cindy Weigand

The label of man-haters turned so many men and women off, particularly in Texas. The crackpots and screwballs you saw on television, that doesn't go over here. You had to be part of the mainstream.

Hermine Tobolowsky

There's a way to do it, and I don't think it's to go in like gang-busters: By God, I'm a woman and you're damn well going to accept me. I think it's: Here I am. I think I can do the job. Give me a chance.

Frances Kaiser

One of the biggest struggles for women today is learning to say no without guilt.

Sheri McConnell

I may believe a lot of things that have been proposed as a feminist philosophy, but I don't believe it as a feminist. It's not that I agree or disagree, it's just that's not the way I want to carry the cause.

Catherine Jean Crier

Every life, no matter how exciting and exalted it may be, is bound together by the trivial and the mundane. It is this very trivia—cooking a meal, doing the laundry, bandaging a skinned knee—that keeps life glued together. It is also this trivia that for some years has been the heart of the women's revolution.

Vivian Castleberry

It never occurred to me not to try to have it all.

Wendy Gramm

I find it refreshing to have at last found my own voice and to speak my own mind.

Louise Raggio

I think women add special dimensions if they're allowed to speak their own voices.

Vivian Castleberry

WRITERS & WRITING

Writers are like knights in shining armor. They constantly battle with words, tame the dragons within structure and plot, rescue the right sentence from the pits of the unruly paragraph monsters. In the end they always win.

Caroline (Karolina) Blaha-Black

I simply want to be free to say what I feel and think exactly as I am able—leave my testament, offer my evidence of what I found in this life.

Katherine Anne Porter

To be complete, to be fulfilled, to be centered—we must tend our soul as lovingly and carefully as we tend the souls of others. We must find the time to turn into our thoughts, our memories, our stories. And we must begin to record those stories.

Susie Kelly Flatau

A professional writer is like a professional athlete—always suited up and ready to play.

Joan R. Neubauer

I've always thought that my literary antecedents were not writers but weavers—what is telling a story but keeping track of those threads?

Sandra Cisneros

Writing practice folds words, simple and exquisite, into everyday stories. Shared reading transforms scribbles into tales universal.

Carlyn Luke Reding

In this time of high speed everything, I consider the ancient form of poetry haiku to be completely modern. If you can't say it in seventeen syllables then don't bother . . . nobody is listening to you anyway.

Jennifer E. Naglieri

In writing you learn to bound back quickly. You jolly well better!
Loula Grace Erdman

What a lot we lost when we stopped writing letters. You can't reread a phone call.

Liz Carpenter

Writing is like jumping off a cliff and trusting the parachute will open when needed.

Stacey Hasbrook

I tell my students that to journal, think "I must write, I must, for how do I know what I think until I see what I say."
Connie L. Williams

Much in writing is a learned skill, but first one must have the creativeness and vocabulary to put thoughts, feelings and facts onto paper and make them a joy to read.
Colleen Greenwood

Start today. Find a sacred space. Gather mementos and memories. Invite life stories to unfold upon your eyelid cinemas. And write. This is your gift to the world.
Susie Kelly Flatau

If our told stories can sweep across our souls like a strong wind, our written stories have hurricane potential!
Susan Wittig Albert

Writing is both a blessing and a curse. Ask anyone who stares at the ceiling all night long, thousands of brilliant words rampaging through their mind like a herd of mad cattle, but cannot put three simple sentences in a line come daylight.
Ginnie Siena Bivona

Poet and poetry unwind ribbons of satin and grosgrain into words and rhythms.

Carlyn Luke Reding

No writing depicts the real problems and triumphs of individuals better than that which is shared in personal letters, journals, and diaries with family and friends.

Vivian Castleberry

Before I could write, I scribbled stories on a Big Chief tablet, and then I re-told the stories to anyone who would listen. I've never quit, but nowadays other people can read my words.

Joan Upton Hall

Talking [about writing] ahead of time takes out all the fizz, like uncorking a bottle of champagne and leaving it standing open.

Loula Grace Erdman

All my past is "usable," in the sense that my material consists of memory, legend, personal experience, and acquired knowledge. They combine in a constant process of re-creation.

Katherine Anne Porter

In all my fiction, I try to explore what it was like to be a woman in the American West, mostly a century ago. I find it works best for me to do that in first person, so that I almost become central figure as well as storyteller.

Judy Alter

I am fascinated by the way pieces of real life combine with bits of chance information, memories, and gifts from the subconscious to make a story. A story is a patchwork quilt from the past.

Annette Sanford

Too many new writers slant their stories, imply opinions not actually stated. In the city-room school of my day, a news reporter was just that —a reporter, not an editorial writer.

Bess Whitehead Scott

Writing fiction you can go into the world where you've never been and make it your own.

Caitlin Kite

Words are things of power, which can crush the human spirit or raise it to new heights.

Guida Jackson

INDEX

N

Z